Introducing Ray FIFO

Hi. I'm Ray FIFO. I'm a Silicon Valley Guy. While the rest of you poor saps are spending the night in cold computer rooms, I'm out there direct-accessing cute little programs at peak transfer rate. Hey! I'm the dude with the moves!

When I first moved to the Valley, I was just like you—a beanie-head fresh out of M.I.T., just aching to get my hands on that Master Core data. Well, that was

fine for a while, that was amusing, and the pay was groovy. But I kept feeling like there was something... missing. I needed another form of stimulation. I finally figured it out, after months of research: What I needed was a relationchip.

So I scanned that new program down in word processing—you know, the one with the huge mammary banks?...Yeah—Ju-lie. Punch my code! I am certain! When I first saw her I thought, Whoa! Give me a microsecond! Could I trip her Kipp relay, or *what?* She sort of smiles at me, and I'm thinking, I have *got* to access this chick. But should I go subroutine or main program, you know? So I just subtly invade her spatial arena and introduce myself for starts...."Hi...I'm Ray FIFO ..."

After a few casual edit statements I can tell this unit really digs me. I mean, it's modem to the max—the program computes, right? We make plans to meet at her place. I get there and she is ON LINE. I mean, like, she's wearing all this software! I'm calculating the access time to her front-end processor, and there is phase jitter entering all my charge-coupled devices. Her ambient temperature's rising, and she is alpha fluxing *right before my eyes!* We skipped dinner...

After a RAM-refresh time interval, she says to me, "Ray—I'm all decoded now. I think you'd better go." And I say, "Okay, Program—I can handle the end sum." "And Ray," she says, "I hope you won't de-rez me in the morning." And I say, "*Moi?* De-rez a cute little program like *you?* Hey! I'm a Silicon Valley Guy!"

THE OFFICIAL

SILICON VALLEY GUY HANDBOOK

PATTY BELL AND DOUG MYRLAND
WITH BOB GLAZAR AS RAY FIFO

**Illustrations and Photographs
by Chucklynn Inc.
Photographs in Chapters 9 and 10
by Bob Glazar**

AVON
PUBLISHERS OF BARD, CAMELOT, DISCUS AND FLARE BOOKS

THE OFFICIAL SILICON VALLEY GUY HANDBOOK
is an original publication of Avon Books.
This work has never before appeared in book form.

AVON BOOKS
A division of
The Hearst Corporation
959 Eighth Avenue
New York, New York 10019

Published by arrangement with the authors
Library of Congress Catalog Card Number: 83-90621
ISBN: 0-380- 84392-7

Library of Congress Cataloging in Publication Data

Bell, Patty.
   The official Silicon Valley guy handbook.

   1. Computer industry—Employees—Anecdotes, facetiae,
satire, etc. I. Myrland, Doug. II. Title.
PN6231.E4B37   1983   818'.5402   83-45132
ISBN 0-380-84392-7

First Avon Printing, June, 1983

Thanks and love to:
Roman and Dolly Ziolkowski
Eli and Eunice Myrland
Chester and Eleanor Glazar
for raising a bunch of bright kids.

Acknowledgments

This is the section of the book where we thank all the people we didn't pay. We're also going to thank a few we *did* pay, because we certainly didn't pay them very much.

Institutional thank-yous go to the Maricopa County Community College District for allowing us to invade their computer center for endless photo sessions; to KMCR-FM Radio for tolerating several

months of craziness and inattention to work; ditto for
Venture Aviation/Arizona Charter Airlines.

Special thanks to all who took time out of their
busy schedules to pose for the interior photos in this
book: Leah "Yes, I Am a Movie Star" Wingfield,
Richard Glazar, Julie Glazar, and Kathy Grundy.

Thanks to Pat Curtis for getting us into the flight-simulator area of a local Air Force Base, and to Norm Dye for possessing a post-holocaust office that looked like we planned it that way.

Thanks to Michael McDonald for his unbridled enthusiasm and help from the very beginning, and to Ken Wingfield for being the most cooperative and creative illustrator anyone ever gave an impossible assignment to. Kathy Grundy gets a real merit badge for organizing, feeding, cajoling, and babysitting us throughout this entire project, not to mention managing the last stages of the operation.

We would also like to thank Jim Todd for his fine photos and for working at a breakneck pace while still retaining his sense of humor. The same goes for Abe Rezny and his assistant, Tommy, for their great work, especially since they had no idea what they were getting into with this bunch.

Greg and Pam Eitzman, Bill Caid, and Jeff Ziolkowski served as real-life SVG inspiration; Pelin Kaylan and Barbara and Tom Neuman provided some inside input and clarification of facts. Thanks also to Paul Robinson.

And then there's Ray FIFO, a.k.a. Bob Glazar, who created the persona of the ultimate Silicon Valley Guy. Bob is a true friend and partner, and he deserves more praise than we have space to give. Thanks, Bob. Thanks one and all.

Contents

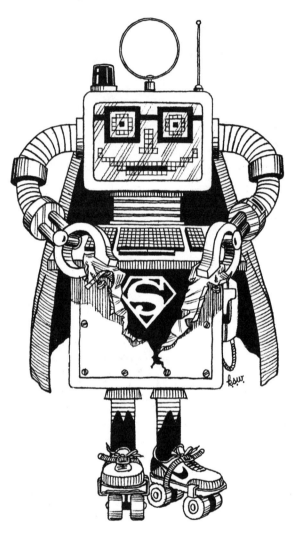

THE OFFICIAL

SILICON
VALLEY GUY
HANDBOOK

Preface

emember when "software" meant T-shirts, and "hardware" was a store down the block? Well, get out your microcomputer dictionary. The Age of the Computer is upon us, bringing with it not only an entirely new vocabulary but new attitudes and modes of dress as well. It's a cultural revolution, the core of which burns whitest in the Silicon Valley.

For more than one hundred years Americans have

traveled to California to find fortune. First the lure was gold. Then the farms and orchards provided fortune for a few and wages for many. The glamor of Hollywood and the sophistication of San Francisco attracted still more seekers. Now, in the epoch that

will someday be called the technological revolution, Americans are drawn to the golden coast by the melding of machine and humanity. They come to worship the computer. They travel to see and even touch the magic chips that make machines "think."

Silicon Valley is that area south of San Francisco encompassed by Santa Clara County. Since the late 1960s, from Palo Alto to San Jose, that region's fruit-growing acres have been gradually overrun by semiconductor companies. What we have here is, as "Adam Smith" called it, "one of the most agreeable provinces of capitalism." What we have here is digital Disneyland.

The men and women who live and work in Silicon Valley are a new breed, citizens of a brave new world. Unlike the rest of us, for whom a computer is just a machine that screws up our bank balance, these people consider a computer a link to reality. They've made the step from using machines to communion with machines. We may smirk at these "Silicon Valley Guys" right now, but soon, probably within our brief lifetimes, the revolution will be so complete as to make those of us who are *not* synergistic with machines the misfits. The engineering and electronics wizards we so fondly outline, exaggerate, and tease in this book are in fact the models for the new-age men and women that our grandchildren certainly will be.

Science-fiction writers need only look just off California State Route 280 to find the characters to populate their futuristic novels. The men and women of Silicon Valley are already experimenting with computer chips designed to be implanted in the human body. And they already have machines that talk, walk, even learn by operant conditioning. We could be frightened by these leaps of science and technology. We choose instead to be fascinated and amused.

1 2 3 4 5 6 7 8 9 10

VIDEO-GAME DESIGNERS

GETTING ON LINE

MARKETING AND MANAGEMENT

11 12

SVG COUPLES

THE WOMEN OF SILICON VALLEY

MAINFRAME FUELING

THE TEEN-AGE SVG

BURNOUT

HEADHUNTING AND JOB-HOPPING

IT'S A DIRTY JOB, BUT SOMEBODY HAS TO DO IT

IF YOU CAN PRONOUNCE IT, DON'T EAT IT

SHOPPING FOR SOFTWARE

HELLO, I MUST BE GOING

COLLEGE DAYS

BRING 'EM IN AND BURN 'EM OUT

EXERCISE

REBEL WITHOUT A COMPILER

YOUR FIRST JOB

LIFE AT THE OLD ALPHA MATER

LIFE IN THE STATE OF HOLY MICROMONY

SHE'LL HAVE FUN, FUN, FUN TILL HER DADDY TAKES HER DISC DRIVE AWAY

HIGH FASHION IN THE HIGH-TECH ENVIRONMENT

AVOIDING THE ARCANE IN THE ARCADE

"ALL I ASK OF MY BODY IS THAT IT CARRY AROUND MY HEAD." —THOMAS ALVA EDISON

It is in high school, during the formative years, that the young SVG first gets the nickname "nerd." And teen-age SVGs *are* nerds as far as their peers are concerned. They're the "Daveys," the kids who carry briefcases to class and get high marks on SATs. Never mind that these nerds have more intelligence packed into one little pinky than the entire senior class; nerds aren't cool, they can't function socially, they can't run with the pack, they weren't born to be wild.

So they are laughed at, socially ostracized, made fun of in the yearbooks. It hurts for a little while, but really doesn't matter much in the big picture, because any nerd worth his salt can see the end sum—that high-paying job waiting for him at Intel as soon as he graduates and gets in a couple of years at M.I.T. Davey *knows* he'll get the last laugh. It's already in the program.

While most teens are spending their free time hanging out and trying not to seem overly intelligent on any subject other than the current fashion trends, the teen-age SVG is learning how to tap into the Bell System's long-distance network. While his peers are learning the Pogo and petting in cars, the "chippie" is in the school electronics shop building a robotic cheerleader that, in looks and voltage output, puts the original to shame. While the other guys are scrawling graffiti on the walls, Mickey Microchip is reprogram-

 Q: How many teen-age SVGs does it take to change a light bulb?

ming the computerized scoreboard to spell out semi-lewd messages for the halftime performance at Friday night's football game.

Parents of normal teen-agers sit up nights waiting to see if their kids come home tipsy or stoned, spouting New Wave philosophies. Parents of teen-age SVGs wait up to see if this week's program was done in BASIC or FORTRAN. It all started with something as simple as a Mr. Wizard Science Kit, but things sure have gone nuts since then.

 **A:** Five.

— One to reroute the high-voltage lines from his neighborhood to Canada, causing a brownout all along the West Coast.

— One to hijack a shipment of arc lamps headed for the Astrodome.

— One to rewire the house with 12-inch coaxial cable.

— One to install the six-ton air handler and cooling system, and:

— One to unscrew the old bulb to substitute the greater light source.

Teen-age SVGs tend to collect a lot of hardware, making their rooms not only a mother's headache but prime ICBM targets as well. From the photocell intrusion detector to the ruby-laser bug dissector, the chippie's room is a treasure house of obscure and dangerous technology adapted to teen-age fantasy. Brothers and sisters of teen-age SVGs tend to run away from home a lot. This is not caused by social maladjustment—it's simple survival instinct. Few, if any, small animals are to be found without telltale scars from electrical hookups in the teen-age SVG's neighborhood.

These years of exploration and experimentation are vital for every young nerd, and thankfully short-lived. Just about the time his family starts thinking about putting him up for adoption or renting him out to Air Research's think tank in Bravo, New Mexico, M.I.T. calls, saying they'd like to stash him away in one of their snug little dormitories on a four-year scholarship. Hails are exchanged all around. Junior gets packed off on a plane to Massachusetts, and Dad immediately calls General Dynamics to come in and clear out the electronics equipment. Several highly sensitive devices are discovered, and Dad gets a "Good Neighbor" check from the government as well as a subpoena from the FBI. This causes all manner of havoc in the household all over again—which only goes to prove there is no definitive answer to the question, "What's a mother to do?"

All right, guys and gals, take out your .05 mechanical pencil by Pentel and take the following quiz. Answers are to be found in the key at the back of the book.

POP QUIZ
Are you SVG material?

1. I invite my friends over to watch
   a. Howard Cosell on Monday nights
   b. *The Thorn Birds*
   c. The girl next door who never draws her curtains
   d. Me work on my computer

2. I take my girl friends to
   a. Barry Manilow concerts
   b. Fellini film festivals
   c. Aspen
   d. Video-game arcades

3. My favorite sport is
   a. Football
   b. Baseball
   c. Basketball
   d. Team appliance rewiring

4. My friends call me
   a. Collect
   b. Irresponsible
   c. In for consultation
   d. Dragon Master

College . . . where academia meets ASCII.* Where the computer time is free and so is lunch, providing you have a properly encoded meal ticket.

The freshman SVG immediately recognizes that college is *his* kind of place. All the forms he's asked to fill out are computerized—meaning he's already got a head start on the liberal arts majors and pre-med enrollees, because he can read and interpret the holes in the keypunch cards. Utilizing this information gets him all the classes he wants, prerequisites not withstanding.

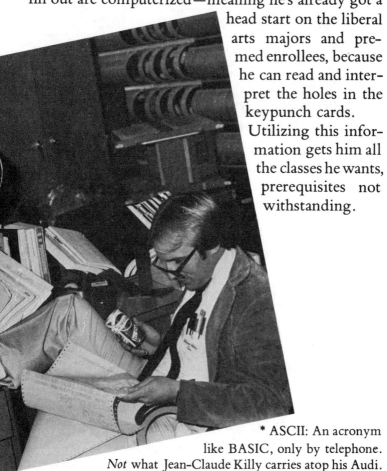

* ASCII: An acronym like BASIC, only by telephone. *Not* what Jean-Claude Killy carries atop his Audi.

At college, freed from parental guidance and curfew laws, young Chip is basically allowed to roam wild about the campus as long as he's completed his class assignments. And when he runs wild, he runs wild—indulging in all sorts of electronically based pranks designed to impress his peers and outwit his professors.

As eagerly as most college freshmen hope to get assigned a dorm room next to the girls' wing, our Chippie prays for a room next to the telephone switching box. Most college initiates hope for work-study in a prominent professor's office, while the SVG student volunteers to keep the computer room clean. When you were in college you probably couldn't have cared less where the next federal grant came from—but if you're a Silicon Valley Guy you'd be concerned because the money might mean the difference between getting a class project designing Spider missiles, or getting a class project studying spiders, period.

Chippies have other chippies for roommates in college. No one else could stand living in the midst of all that electronic clutter and the sea of printout materials. Some colleges try to prevent "cliqueing" by deliberately mixing roommates of different majors. The end result of applying that to chippies is ten or twelve roommates per semester.

College life solidifies the SVG's character and interconnects him with a network of like-minded youths. This has both advantages and disadvantages. On one hand, it is extremely beneficial for him to learn that he is not the only individual on the entire face of the planet Earth who has had to go through the formative years being called a nerd. On the other hand, assembling even small groups of SVGs in the freedom of the college atmosphere can lead to collusion to undermine the basis of the educational structure. The chippie's inquiring mind and sense of adventure at this stage in life usually combine to insure that the college's master computer will be reprogrammed to make each semester two weeks long, do away with final exams, and guarantee each student passing grades.

After four years of lettering in Video Games, the chippie starts to look forward to the future. Dad advises shooting for Motorola, but Mom reminds him Intel has a nicer logo and puts up prettier office buildings. This information is only marginally listened to, because Chip has already decided where he's going: out to Silicon Valley, where the bucks are big and the hot tubs stay open all night.

POP QUIZ
Are you SVG material?

1. I'd like to teach the world to
   a. Sing
   b. Pay its bills
   c. Leave me alone
   d. Reprocess economics programs

2. Girls make the best
   a. Chocolate chip cookies
   b. Mothers
   c. Movie dates
   d. Word processors

3. For Christmas, I bought my mother a
   a. Mood ring
   b. Smoke alarm
   c. Fur coat
   d. Telephone coupler

1 2 **3** 4 5 6 7 8 9 10

VIDEO-GAME DESIGNERS

GETTING ON LINE

MARKETING AND MANAGEMENT

11 12

SVG COUPLES

THE WOMEN OF SILICON VALLEY

MAINFRAME FUELING

THE TEEN-AGE SVG

BURNOUT

HEADHUNTING AND JOB-HOPPING

IT'S A DIRTY JOB, BUT SOMEBODY HAS TO DO IT

IF YOU CAN PRONOUNCE IT, DON'T EAT IT

SHOPPING FOR SOFTWARE

HELLO, I MUST BE GOING

COLLEGE DAYS

BRING 'EM IN AND BURN 'EM OUT

EXERCISE

REBEL WITHOUT A COMPILER

YOUR FIRST JOB

LIFE AT THE OLD ALPHA MATER

LIFE IN THE STATE OF HOLY MICROMONY

SHE'LL HAVE FUN, FUN, FUN TILL HER DADDY TAKES HER DISC DRIVE AWAY

HIGH FASHION IN THE HIGH-TECH ENVIRONMENT

AVOIDING THE ARCANE IN THE ARCADE

"ALL I ASK OF MY BODY IS THAT IT CARRY AROUND MY HEAD." —THOMAS ALVA EDISON

This is it. Fresh out of college, you've been hired by a multinational computer firm in Silicon Valley. Following a map drawn hastily by the hyperactive recruiter, you drive your Honda Accord into the parking lot, then head for the build-

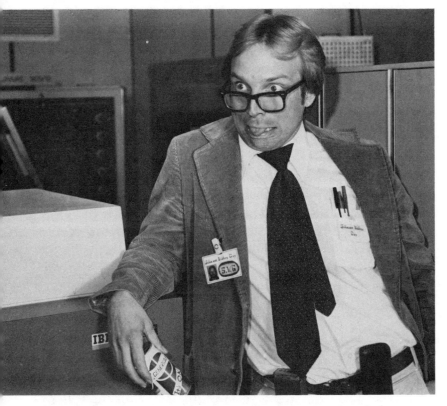

ing. From the moment you hear the *whoosh* of the electronic doors and the jangle of keys on the security guard's belt, you feel at home. Just like Dorothy Kilgallen, you enter and sign in, please.

Orientation is preprogrammed. Your picture is

taken for your ID badge, you're given a bumper sticker for your car and an identifying access number to the main computer. You are shown around by a representative from the Human Resources Department who hands you a printout of company activities: volleyball game schedules, the hours the hot tubs are open, a map to the person's house who's holding the weekend beer bash. You note that the company cafeteria has more vending machines than you've ever seen in your life. You meet an engineer who tells you on the sly how to tap into the ongoing Adventures game. Then, suddenly, there you are alone in your modular office unit. So, what's next?

Good advice for starting any new job in the computer industry is: Get to Know Your Terminal. Is it user-friendly? Are there sharp edges? If you get your nose too close to the print head, will it catch and drag your face across two reams of printout before you're saved by END OF LINE? Are there shock hazards if you try to retrieve your pencil from beneath the keyboard? Will the terminal house your secret reprogramming of Missile Command?

And while you're about it, you should also get to know your chair. For instance, find out, early on, just how far back you can lean before you experience a total system dump.

The next step is to carefully peer over the wall of your modular office unit and see what your wall mate is up to. **Caution:** Do not attempt verbal contact at first. In some companies it is considered socially unacceptable to communicate by means other than via your terminals.

Check out your wall mate's environment. Is his terminal on? Is his chalkboard full of meaningless mathematical scribbles? Is his IN basket full of printouts and candy wrappers? If so, you can feel confident your new neighbor is an SVG just like you.

If, however, the desk is in pristine order, with the telephone in a prominent position and the terminal off, you can be pretty sure this guy or gal is bucking for management. Proceed with extreme caution in any endeavors to contact them either verbally or by electronic means.

Perhaps your wall mate fits in neither of these two categories. Perhaps, if you are extemely lucky, your wall mate's cubicle will look like this:

1. Cat calendar on wall.

2. Coffee cup with bunnies and/or lions on coaster on desk.

3. Bud vase with silk flowers next to terminal.

4. Complicated-looking telephone with extra buttons on desk.

5. Pillow in chair.

If the cubicle next to yours looks like this, you have been placed in the high-rent district of office modules. You're situated next to a processing technician—a team secretary—a mom substitute who'll take such good care of you that life in your office will be the next best thing to coming home for Thanksgiving.

After you've observed the layout of the modular work units and discovered the occupancy of your neighbor's, it's time to explore your own cubicle more fully. Check the floor for electrical outlets. Decide where you'll plug in your hot comb and your Heathkit electrosonic air-ionizer/soup warmer for those marathon debugging sessions.

Also: Experiment with your phone. Does the company have a WATS line? Can you conference-call enough players to get a good game of Dungeons and Dragons going? Can you conference-call overseas to include your friend in Saudi Arabia who has just invented a new D&D called Mosques and Camels?

Once you are satisfied your new accommodations will do, set your mainframe down in front of your terminal, access some energy, and write, "Hi...I'm Ray FIFO..."

POP QUIZ
Are you SVG material?

1. Home is where
   a. I hang my hat
   b. The heart is
   c. My folks live
   d. I keep my Heathkit catalogues

2. My favorite television show is
   a. *Sesame Street*
   b. *The Honeymooners* reruns
   c. *Saturday Night Live*
   d. Horizontal lines

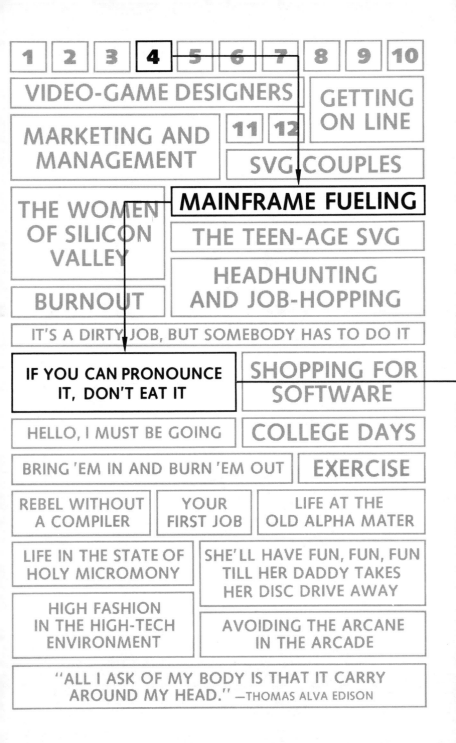

1 2 3 **4** 5 6 7 8 9 10

VIDEO-GAME DESIGNERS

GETTING ON LINE

MARKETING AND MANAGEMENT

11 12

SVG COUPLES

MAINFRAME FUELING

THE WOMEN OF SILICON VALLEY

THE TEEN-AGE SVG

HEADHUNTING AND JOB-HOPPING

BURNOUT

IT'S A DIRTY JOB, BUT SOMEBODY HAS TO DO IT

IF YOU CAN PRONOUNCE IT, DON'T EAT IT

SHOPPING FOR SOFTWARE

HELLO, I MUST BE GOING

COLLEGE DAYS

BRING 'EM IN AND BURN 'EM OUT

EXERCISE

REBEL WITHOUT A COMPILER

YOUR FIRST JOB

LIFE AT THE OLD ALPHA MATER

LIFE IN THE STATE OF HOLY MICROMONY

SHE'LL HAVE FUN, FUN, FUN TILL HER DADDY TAKES HER DISC DRIVE AWAY

HIGH FASHION IN THE HIGH-TECH ENVIRONMENT

AVOIDING THE ARCANE IN THE ARCADE

"ALL I ASK OF MY BODY IS THAT IT CARRY AROUND MY HEAD." —THOMAS ALVA EDISON

When a Silicon Valley Guy says, "Let's do lunch!" he usually means meet him in front of the vending machines in the company cafeteria. Processed food is the staple diet of SVGs. By adulthood a delicate chemical balance has been established that can be maintained only by the most careful procurement and ingestion of proper foodstuffs. In keeping with the usual paternalistic attitude of most computer companies, food suitable for SVG consumption is made available during the work week. Considering that most SVGs spend ninety-five percent of their lives at work, it is not too far-fetched to assume that many of them don't have to face the problem of obtaining food from sources other than vending machines for months at a time.

Knowing just when to eat is a big enough problem for many SVGs; chippies rarely take up much cortex memory space with nutritional information. Some find it helpful to memorize a few key concepts related to feeling faint and fueling their mainframes, and let it go at that. The following has proved helpful in some of the more drastic cases:

Step One: Think of a Radio Shack.

Step Two: Think of a Radio Shack that sells only batteries—a Battery Shack.

Step Three: Think of your body as a high-drain, low-efficiency calculator.

Step Four: Think of a grocery store as a Battery Shack for your body.

SVGs can relate to these concepts, and soon begin to realize that a Hungry Man dinner is to the human body what a 220-volt power line is to the company mainframe.

Locating the grocery store most likely to cater to SVG needs is essential. Signs advertising "Our New Deli Section" indicate that either the store has an over-abundance of non–chemically treated foods or a clientele that wears saris and worships elephants. "Gourmet" markets should be avoided at all costs. Such places are likely to have piles of superfluous and distracting fresh vegetables and only a limited supply, if any, of the factory-processed foods so necessary for maintaining the correct octane level of your bloodstream. Instead, find a user-friendly store: one which has entered the electronic age with a smoothly operating optical sensor on the door and a checkout section which utilizes Universal Product Code readers and voice-synthesis price calling.

After gaining entry into the store, the shopping foray can begin. SVGs choose certain kinds of foods over others for two basic reasons:

> 1.   It has the familiar look of something that can be purchased from a machine.
>
> 2.   The photo representation on the label assures him the contents have no resemblance to something that was once alive.

SVGs avoid any food with recognizable appendages such as legs, wings, or heads, as this food will likely require inordinate amounts of processing and heat sterilization before consumption, and probably doesn't have much chemical content anyway.

We all get a little confused at the grocery store from time to time, confronted as we are with such an endless variety of items to choose from. When in doubt, the wise SVG shopper goes for food that is roughly the color of some familiar plastic object, or which lists monosodium glutamate among the first three items on the "ingredients" label.

Almost every SVG eventually develops a reasonable level of efficiency at exchanging monetary units for food. But he certainly looks forward to the day when the company cafeteria is open on holidays, and vending machines are as plentiful as mailboxes.

POP QUIZ
Are you SVG material?

1. My favorite section of the grocery store is the
   a. Frozen food department
   b. Liquor section
   c. Veggie bins
   d. The Universal Product Code reader

2. When waiting in line at the grocery store checkout counter I read
   a. *The National Enquirer*
   b. *People* magazine
   c. *Reader's Digest*
   d. The Universal Product Codes on my food—and on my magazines

1 2 3 4 **5** 6 7 8 9 10

VIDEO-GAME DESIGNERS

GETTING ON LINE

MARKETING AND MANAGEMENT

11 12

SVG COUPLES

THE WOMEN OF SILICON VALLEY

MAINFRAME FUELING

THE TEEN-AGE SVG

BURNOUT

HEADHUNTING AND JOB-HOPPING

IT'S A DIRTY JOB, BUT SOMEBODY HAS TO DO IT

IF YOU CAN PRONOUNCE IT, DON'T EAT IT

SHOPPING FOR SOFTWARE

HELLO, I MUST BE GOING

COLLEGE DAYS

BRING 'EM IN AND BURN 'EM OUT

EXERCISE

REBEL WITHOUT A COMPILER

YOUR FIRST JOB

LIFE AT THE OLD ALPHA MATER

LIFE IN THE STATE OF HOLY MICROMONY

SHE'LL HAVE FUN, FUN, FUN TILL HER DADDY TAKES HER DISC DRIVE AWAY

HIGH FASHION IN THE HIGH-TECH ENVIRONMENT

AVOIDING THE ARCANE IN THE ARCADE

"ALL I ASK OF MY BODY IS THAT IT CARRY AROUND MY HEAD." —THOMAS ALVA EDISON

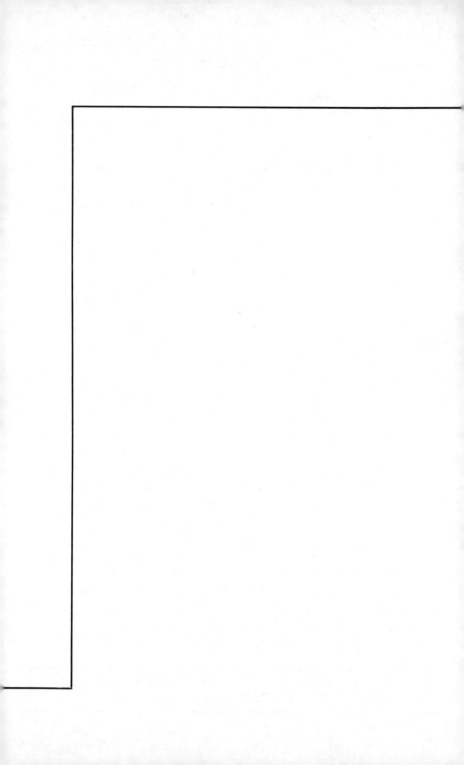

One look at the physique of any given SVG will tell you that exercise, or maintaining the personal mainframe, is not exactly a top priority program. Considering the nature of his work, the average SVG tends to have a lot of LED in his backside. We can see you now—looking around, saying, "Who? Me?"

Chances are you got plenty of exercise when you were only a mere microchip. Remember walking twenty-six blocks to the Radio Shack? Remember climbing telephone poles to find that giant transformer you needed for your antitank missile? Remember tunneling under your street to place the parabolic microphone under your neighbor's rec room?

Those days are gone, wiz-kid! You know the most exercise you get now is quick-thumbing *Computerworld*. Face it, if Richard Simmons were a Silicon Valley Guy, he'd still be a tubbo.

So reprogramming your life-style may be necessary. But take heart and don't dump all the floppies yet. You've already got the basics for an appropriate exercise program; all that's needed is a little modification to the data.

Probably the most immediately helpful advice we can give you for getting started on this program is: Remember to move your legs at least once every eight hours. Occasionally leave your terminal and mobilize your mainframe outside the confines of your think tank. This will insure that your cortex remains in communication with the outer extremities of your mainframe hardware.

We hesitate to advocate anything as strenuous as joining the company volleyball team at this point, but in preparation for that eventuality we suggest the following:

1. *Isometrics:* Place hands on sides of terminal and press in. Hold this for as long as it takes the print head to output fifty copies of your résumé.

2. *Cleaning your modular office unit:* Just locating and gathering up all the empty cola cans should give you plenty of bend and stretch moves.

3. *Finding your car in the parking lot:* Park in an unfamiliar parking place in the morning. Upon leaving work in the evening you will

have forgotten where you parked, forcing you to get in plenty of walking as you wander around searching for your vehicle.

Truly dedicated SVGs have been known to even forget to breathe, especially when waiting for their terminal to read out data or while debugging an IC board. This forgetfulness can lead to phase jitter and can easily be prevented. Simply program your firmware to substitute the word "breathe" for END OF LINE as a sort of reminder. Then once every hour or so have your terminal run a continuous END OF LINE statement for about five minutes. Not only is this great for your cardiopulmonary system, but it occasionally leads to hyperventilation, which can result in getting you a nice little much-needed nap.

POP QUIZ
Are you SVG material?

1. I cross
   a. Intersections
   b. Borders
   c. Insensitive people
   d. ICs

2. The most expensive thing in my bathroom is
   a. The rug
   b. The hair dryer
   c. The designer towels
   d. The voltmeter

Clothes make the man, everywhere but in Silicon Valley. Here almost everyone dresses alike, and not very tastefully at that. "Fashion" is not a term indigenous to the double-E major's vocabulary. Generally, the look is comfortable crumpled cotton, with no cute dangly things to get caught in high-speed print heads.

There are certain style prerequisites, though. For example, an ample breast pocket in the button-down-collared white cotton shirt is essential, given the stress factor of a typically loaded and functional pocket protector. Belt loops on the pants are a must, for a belt needs loops and a beeper needs a belt from which to hang. Pants should be long enough to clear the knees, yet short enough to provide easy access to the tennis-shoe tops. Underwear is optional, as are socks; but should either be purchased, they should be one hundred percent cotton and white.

Shopping for clothes isn't easy for most of us, considering current fashion trends and the downswing in the economy, but for the SVG the process is extremely simple. Only three basic questions need be considered when looking for suitable mainframe drapings:

1.   Am I cold?

2.   Am I a boy or a girl?

3.   Does this store sell clothes?

If the answer to No. 1 is "yes," that means sweaters or long-sleeved T-shirts are in order. The answer to No. 2

determines the color of the sweaters or T-shirts to be purchased. Figuring out No. 3 beforehand will save you the social embarrassment of absentmindedly approaching a Radio Shack salesman and saying, "Excuse me—could you show me something in a beige polyester leisure suit?"

Experience proves that large discount stores are the best bet for finding correct clothes for chippies. The smell of popcorn, coupled with a high-distortion PA system announcing Blue Light Specials, assures you this establishment has a full line of SVG fashions. All the software here is prepackaged, an aesthetically pleasing concept for the time-pressed. Grab your garb and go, as it were.

For the slightly more discriminating, one might shop the local department stores. These establishments have software monitors (salespersons) who are quite ready and willing to advise you on the appropriateness of your purchases. Beware, however, the software monitors who advocate flannel (too fuzzy for clean-room work) or stretch denim (appealing static cling, but dangerous around soldering materials). Look instead for an SM who's into pure fabrics and who *likes* the way your pant cuffs hover around your ankles.

Purchasing custom software (tailor-made clothing) can be immediately dismissed as too costly and time-consuming. One has to return to the software designers again and again for debugging, and the final product usually has at least one residual bug (straight pin) that you will only discover the first time you set your mainframe down wearing that outfit.

Taking all this into consideration, choose your

favorite stuff and buy six of everything, preferably in the same color. (Buying in monotone saves time sorting colors at the laundromat. You know what a laundromat is—it's that place that has rows of machines that look like coin-operated disc drives.) Pay for your purchases with one of your plastic monetary-exchange cards, and leave the store feeling confident that not only have you interfaced with interfacing, but you've covered your baud as well.

POP QUIZ
Are you SVG material?

1. For formal affairs I dress in
   a. Costumes of foreign lands
   b. Polyester
   c. Something clean
   d. BASIC black

2. The SVG's closet is organized by
   a. Season
   b. Color
   c. Day of the week
   d. Pile

| 1 | 2 | 3 | 4 | 5 | 6 | **7** | 8 | 9 | 10 |

VIDEO-GAME DESIGNERS

GETTING ON LINE

MARKETING AND MANAGEMENT

| 11 | 12 |

SVG COUPLES

THE WOMEN OF SILICON VALLEY

MAINFRAME FUELING

THE TEEN-AGE SVG

BURNOUT

HEADHUNTING AND JOB-HOPPING

IT'S A DIRTY JOB, BUT SOMEBODY HAS TO DO IT

IF YOU CAN PRONOUNCE IT, DON'T EAT IT

SHOPPING FOR SOFTWARE

HELLO, I MUST BE GOING

COLLEGE DAYS

BRING 'EM IN AND BURN 'EM OUT

EXERCISE

REBEL WITHOUT A COMPILER

YOUR FIRST JOB

LIFE AT THE OLD ALPHA MATER

LIFE IN THE STATE OF HOLY MICROMONY

SHE'LL HAVE FUN, FUN, FUN TILL HER DADDY TAKES HER DISC DRIVE AWAY

HIGH FASHION IN THE HIGH-TECH ENVIRONMENT

AVOIDING THE ARCANE IN THE ARCADE

"ALL I ASK OF MY BODY IS THAT IT CARRY AROUND MY HEAD." —THOMAS ALVA EDISON

The computer industry has never been accused of discrimination on the basis of sex. Here, if you've got the brains, you get the bytes. There's only one important thing to say about the female aspect of the Silicon Valley type:

The Silicon Valley Girl is simply a Silicon Valley Guy with longer hair and smaller feet.

POP QUIZ
Are you SVG material?

1. My first crush was on
   a. Daddy
   b. Andy Gibb
   c. Burt Reynolds
   d. Mr. Wizard

2. I never carry
   a. Mace
   b. Herpes
   c. Tic–Tacs
   d. A depowered beeper

3. I am most afraid of
   a. Norman Bates
   b. Tylenol
   c. Telling my mother I'm sleeping with a person from a different religious persuasion
   d. De-rezzing my own program

4. Come...
   a. Up and see me some time
   b. Here
   c. uppance
   d. puter

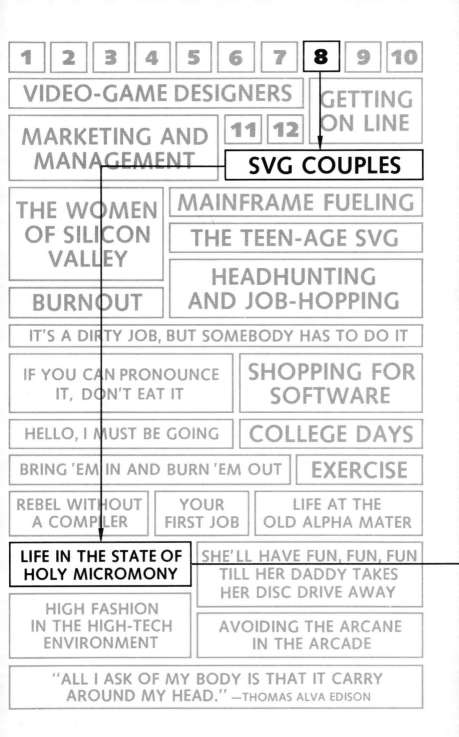

| 1 | 2 | 3 | 4 | 5 | 6 | 7 | **8** | 9 | 10 |

VIDEO-GAME DESIGNERS

GETTING ON LINE

MARKETING AND MANAGEMENT

| 11 | 12 |

SVG COUPLES

THE WOMEN OF SILICON VALLEY

MAINFRAME FUELING

THE TEEN-AGE SVG

BURNOUT

HEADHUNTING AND JOB-HOPPING

IT'S A DIRTY JOB, BUT SOMEBODY HAS TO DO IT

IF YOU CAN PRONOUNCE IT, DON'T EAT IT

SHOPPING FOR SOFTWARE

HELLO, I MUST BE GOING

COLLEGE DAYS

BRING 'EM IN AND BURN 'EM OUT

EXERCISE

REBEL WITHOUT A COMPILER

YOUR FIRST JOB

LIFE AT THE OLD ALPHA MATER

LIFE IN THE STATE OF HOLY MICROMONY

SHE'LL HAVE FUN, FUN, FUN TILL HER DADDY TAKES HER DISC DRIVE AWAY

HIGH FASHION IN THE HIGH-TECH ENVIRONMENT

AVOIDING THE ARCANE IN THE ARCADE

"ALL I ASK OF MY BODY IS THAT IT CARRY AROUND MY HEAD." —THOMAS ALVA EDISON

They probably met in the computer room in college. Perhaps they were assigned to share a modem in Programming 250, or maybe they just looked up from their respective terminals and noticed they were the only two left in the computer lab at midnight. A few casual edit statements turn into a marathon conversation and social interaction. A mutual-admiration society is formed, the logical conclusion of which is—you guessed it—marriage.

Even though most facets of the computer business seem oriented toward the single person, couples are proliferating. They are the inevitable result of an educational and industrial system that throws together

young innocents
of both sexes without regard to
emotional stability or vulnerability.

Unlike most married couples, SVG couples put very little work or effort into their marriages. Not because they're not willing, but because both halves of this union have no skills other than those relating to machines with tiny chips for brains and keyboards for ears. These folks are in deep trouble: Their lives are all too often an ongoing period of adjustment, with one perplexing event after another.

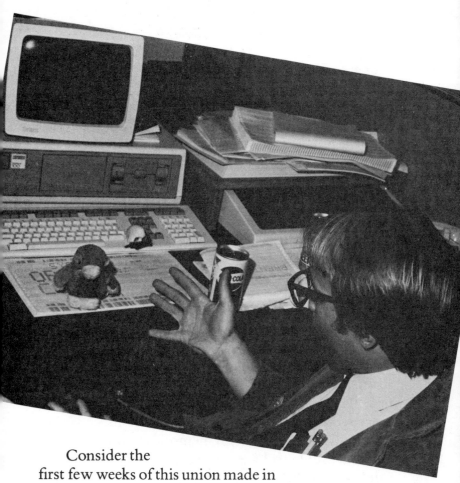

Consider the
first few weeks of this union made in
UNIVAC heaven. While the honeymoon period is
typically one of blissful relaxation, for the computer
couple it is most probably a series of disorienting
events followed by a shocking cutoff from high
technology. The usual honeymoon cabin in the
Poconos has no terminal. It has no floppy discs. Its
structure consists of logs and beams, rather than
logarithms and ICs. In this atmosphere of panoramic
views, fireplaces, and heart-shaped bathtubs, the SVG

couple finds their only comfort in the knowledge that at least the phone is a touch-tone model, and given enough time, they could access some computer somewhere through the Bell System. Once they gratefully leave the honeymoon lodge and return to the Valley to set up housekeeping, things usually get worse.

Considering that the typical Computer Science major has no training or experience dealing with the world of house-hunting, establishing credit, or even locating his/her own food, the SVG couple's experiences in the early months of marriage are not surprising. They sometimes have a vague notion that they are supposed to take on different roles, but they have no idea what roles, let alone why. Observations of the way their parents conducted their lives were probably casual and sporadic. Much more important were their own benchmark experiences (their calculus and advanced math classes, their first digital watch, their first 10,000,000 points on a Space Command game). In other words, their childhood observations of family life are all too colored with memories of diodes, resistors and LEDs to have any sociological accuracy or validity. So they struggle. They *try* to remember how Mom cooked dinner and Dad mowed the lawn, but the results are usually just a sort of humorous and blundering attempt at facsimile.

These young couples don't search for their identity; they have trouble just finding their way home. They don't have mid-life crises, because they burn out before they reach mid-life. We've all known couples who were similar in size, and so occasionally wore each other's shirts or slacks. These couples wear each other's clothes no matter *what* size they are, because they lack the aesthetic judgment to tell the difference between a pants suit and a pack of huskies.

Despite these intrinsic problems, a clear majority of Silicon Valley couples are happy in their ignorance. Once adjusted to cohabitation, they blissfully spend their days together sitting side by side in their electronically monitored jacuzzis, sharing the keyboards of their home terminals, and double-trunking their modems even as they're double-bunking in the bedroom. And speaking of the bedroom—propriety prevents too much detail, but let us say that while the discovery of sex often comes as both a delightful surprise and a mild inconvenience to these young moderns, they usually find a way to preprogram their firmware so as to simulate a reasonably amorous and predictable sex life.

These couples sometimes have children, but usually only after they've suffered mutual burnout around the age of thirty-five. At that point in their lives, these couples either rise to mid- or upper management together, never to be heard from again, or they withdraw their profit-sharing money, have babies, and move to a trailer park in Lodi where they spend the rest of their days weaving macrame out of multi-par cables and eating natural foods.

POP QUIZ
Are you SVG material?

1. I want a girl, just like the girl who ...
    a. Works in the Playboy Club
    b. Married dear old Dad
    c. Married Prince Charles
    d. Works in word processing

2. If ever I would leave you, it wouldn't be in
    a. Summer
    b. Burbank
    c. Trouble
    d. The middle of a debugging project

3. Never a dull
    a. Moment
    b. Minute
    c. Knife
    d. Microsecond

4. My favorite name for a small child is
    a. Barbie
    b. Ken
    c. Zippy the Pin Head
    d. HAL

| 1 | 2 | 3 | 4 | 5 | 6 | 7 | 8 | **9** | 10 |

VIDEO-GAME DESIGNERS

GETTING ON LINE

MARKETING AND MANAGEMENT

| 11 | 12 |

SVG COUPLES

THE WOMEN OF SILICON VALLEY

MAINFRAME FUELING

THE TEEN-AGE SVG

BURNOUT

HEADHUNTING AND JOB-HOPPING

IT'S A DIRTY JOB, BUT SOMEBODY HAS TO DO IT

IF YOU CAN PRONOUNCE IT, DON'T EAT IT

SHOPPING FOR SOFTWARE

HELLO, I MUST BE GOING

COLLEGE DAYS

BRING 'EM IN AND BURN 'EM OUT

EXERCISE

REBEL WITHOUT A COMPILER

YOUR FIRST JOB

LIFE AT THE OLD ALPHA MATER

LIFE IN THE STATE OF HOLY MICROMONY

SHE'LL HAVE FUN, FUN, FUN TILL HER DADDY TAKES HER DISC DRIVE AWAY

HIGH FASHION IN THE HIGH-TECH ENVIRONMENT

AVOIDING THE ARCANE IN THE ARCADE

"ALL I ASK OF MY BODY IS THAT IT CARRY AROUND MY HEAD." —THOMAS ALVA EDISON

nly two kinds of human beings can success-
fully play video games:

1. Those under the age of fifteen.
2. The SVGs who design them.

Synergy with machines that imitate mass destruc-
tion is easy to understand in children. After all, they
have none of the political enlightenment we adults
have, they're in the throes of discovering the limitless
boundaries of their own personal power bases, and
they could care less where the quarters come from as
long as they can keep on guiding Pac-Man through his
neon-colored maze.

Much the same sort of logic applies to SVGs.
They are unlike any other class of adult with respon-
sibilities, since the all-powerful Mother Company
usually takes care of basic needs and even occasionally
forces a bit of group recreation on its wards. As to
where the quarters come from, that's often a difficult
concept for SVGs—Economic Theory is not a core
course for Computer Science majors. Never mind that
at Activision the board time is free, twenty-four hours
a day.

Every SVG is a potential vid-game designer—
some just take it more seriously than others and
specifically ask to be transferred to those departments
in the companies that can utilize their talents best. The
peculiar psychology that motivates these intergalactic-
war simulators is difficult, if not impossible, to understand. We criticize the Libyans for teaching their Third
World children how to march and salute, and then we

proceed to supply *our* little angels with tokens to shoot off imaginary ICBMs. The ladies and gentlemen of Silicon Valley are concerned primarily with finding new and more challenging games, not international harmony.

Living on caffeine and Oh Henry bars for six weeks at a stretch can create some really bizarre mental images for anyone, let alone one of our vid-oriented SVGs. Just think about the Master Control who created Pac-Man. What combination of late-night hours coupled with a diet of preservative-packed junk foods caused an otherwise sane man to turn a smiley face to profile and race it around an allegorical highway in search of food and ghosts? What perverse media memories made another renegade SVG want to recreate the Louis–Schmeling fight with an ape and a carpenter?

The life of a vid-game designer is not an easy one. Just when the electronics wizard thinks he's created the final challenge, some smart-ass ten-year-old shoots down 80,000,000 alien vessels with one quarter, stopping only because the weekend is almost over and he has to go home and finish his schoolwork. No rest is in sight for these select members of the new master race, since every kid with a quarter is the potential Rocky of the arcade.

Vid-game designers are always on the lookout for inspiration. Pigeons in the park become giant birds of prey feasting on members of a space colony in the Orion galaxy. Cars on the freeway become malevolent insects tunneling through a moon of Jupiter. Some vid-game designers have been known to take drugs, but the horrible truth is that the stimulus that produces these mind/machine perversions is normally no more than six cans of cola and a jelly doughnut.

As a child, the designer liked to turn the color-TV controls to "splatter" in order to intensify the experience. These people don't wash the bugs off their windshield because they like the patterns they make.

And they dress even funnier than regular SVGs. Hawaiian shirts and Danskin body stockings have been seen on the females; *Star Trek* T-shirts are common for the males. Corneas of varying colors occur with regularity in this special breed.

Typically, a vid–game designer was the organizer of the local Trekkie chapter of his college. He or she probably reprogrammed the high-school scoreboard to read "War is imminent! Take to the hills!" at halftime.

As with every other SVG, burnout can be expected around the age of thirty-five. Retirement possibilities include operating the Space Mountain ride at Disneyland or counting cars for the state highway department. Many choose a second career in the demolition derby, and a goodly number become politicians. Female vid-game retirees often find work in school cafeterias, where their fondness for bizarre color combinations is greatly appreciated. On the superhighway of Silicon Valley life, these video-game designers deserve a big round of applause for staying in the passing lane all the way to the end of the electronic interstate.

POP QUIZ
Are you vid-game designer material?

1. Buzz is
   a. A sound bees make
   b. A feeling you have after doing drugs
   c. Something pilots do to herds of sheep
   d. My nickname

2. As a small child I liked to play
   a. Doctor and Nurse
   b. Cowboys and Indians
   c. Hide and Seek
   d. Master Control and Robot

3. Where there's smoke, there's
   a. Fire
   b. Drugs
   c. Indians sending signals
   d. A defective circuit board

4. My favorite conversation topic with new acquaintances is to ask them where they
   a. Get their cars detailed
   b. Play tennis
   c. Jog
   d. Find the best soldering materials

1 2 3 4 5 6 7 8 9 **10**

VIDEO-GAME DESIGNERS

GETTING ON LINE

MARKETING AND MANAGEMENT

11 12

SVG COUPLES

THE WOMEN OF SILICON VALLEY

MAINFRAME FUELING

THE TEEN-AGE SVG

BURNOUT

HEADHUNTING AND JOB-HOPPING

IT'S A DIRTY JOB, BUT SOMEBODY HAS TO DO IT

IF YOU CAN PRONOUNCE IT, DON'T EAT IT

SHOPPING FOR SOFTWARE

HELLO, I MUST BE GOING

COLLEGE DAYS

BRING 'EM IN AND BURN 'EM OUT

EXERCISE

REBEL WITHOUT A COMPILER

YOUR FIRST JOB

LIFE AT THE OLD ALPHA MATER

LIFE IN THE STATE OF HOLY MICROMONY

SHE'LL HAVE FUN, FUN, FUN TILL HER DADDY TAKES HER DISC DRIVE AWAY

HIGH FASHION IN THE HIGH-TECH ENVIRONMENT

AVOIDING THE ARCANE IN THE ARCADE

"ALL I ASK OF MY BODY IS THAT IT CARRY AROUND MY HEAD." —THOMAS ALVA EDISON

Real Silicon Valley Guys and Girls don't go into marketing or management. This is a truism that has proven itself repeatedly in the history of the computer business. A dedicated senior chippie aspires to nothing more than a corner-situated modular office unit and a level-one code book inscribed with

his initials. The idea of doing something all day long that involves actual contact with the general public is anathema.

Nonetheless, these jobs must be filled. And they're filled by people for whom a mainframe is nothing more than what goes around their Leroy

Neiman painting. They think terminal refers to a ward in a hospital. These executroids have even been known to iron their clothes and buy pants that have no belt loops! How do they carry their beepers? How can you wear a plastic pocket protector on a shirt that has no pocket?

These folks may have gone to electronics school, but chances are they chose the school for the social life rather than the core memory of the college computer. These are the razor-cut fraternity types and blow-dried sorority girls who sat in the back of the class and asked questions like, "Can I write an essay instead of debugging the program?" These *pseudo* Silicon Valley Guys and Girls (hereafter referred to as PSVGs) are often so distracted by the outside world and the company-provided recreational opportunities that they let their terminal keyboards get dusty.

The uninitiated outside world often mistakes (briefly) the PSVGs for the genuine article. So that you won't do the same, we offer you the seven warning signs of a PSVG:

1. Louis Vuitton briefcases.

2. Contact lenses.

3. Shoes made from creatures that were once alive.

4. Clothes that have "dry-clean only" tags.

5. Ordering Perrier and hors d'oeuvres.

6. Reading *The Wall Street Journal*.

7. Possession of a Club Med card.

Within the PSVG fiefdom are two divisions: Management and Marketing. A real SVG never thinks of "management" without the word "database" preceding it. He never thinks of "marketing" without free-associating Universal Product Code readers and frozen pizza. Management, to the PSVG, however, means being part of a *Fortune* 500 company and smoking Tiparillos with Lee Van Cleef. Marketing, to the PSVG, means convincing the general public that their checking accounts would balance and their kids would go to the head of their class if only they had a microcomputer in every bathroom.

To both of these factions, M&M means perks. Not regular SVG perks, like coupons good at Burger King, but *real* perks: like houses and expensive foreign cars and grooming services for their Lhasa Apsos. The more important the project, the larger the perk.

Management-category PSVGs tend to travel a lot, quite often in the company jet. They meet with Japanese businessmen in strange places like Singapore and Waco, Texas. Management types fancy themselves to be SVGs with savvy, but in reality they are simply what they are: Management types. The first people they usually see when they step out of their planes are the Marketing types. The Marketing PSVGs like to toady to their bosses.

Marketing PSVGs get their Walkman units confused with their beepers. They buy ornate little frames for their company ID badges and then leave them at home on the dresser because "it spoils the lines of my blouse." While real SVGs live in apartment complexes in Mountain View and Sunnydale, Marketing types live in "an upscale target market in a primary demographic," which means they live in the better part of Palo Alto where the people buy food processors and have juvenile delinquents for children.

SVGs watch television by accident, when their Atari fritzes out. Management PSVGs deliberately

watch *Wall Street Week.* Marketing PSVGs watch the competition's commercials and Phil Donahue.

As children, the Management types were the ones who squealed to the teacher when the chippies rewired the school clocks to let everyone out an hour early. The kids who grew up to be Marketing types would have squealed too, except they were too busy digging through the wastebasket in the teacher's lounge looking for potential blackmail material to have time to fink on their peers.

And last, but not least, M&M PSVGs make money—lots of it—megabucks!—while the real SVGs

labor over hot terminals and debug the programs that put those very megabucks into the pockets of the upper-echelon employees. It's just like your System Data Bus—your higher-priority masters have control of the vehicle, and the slaves move to the back of the Bus.

POP QUIZ
Are you PSVG material?

1. All roads lead to
   a. More roads
   b. Thrifty Mart
   c. Mom's house
   d. Palo Alto

2. As a child I liked to play
   a. House
   b. With matches
   c. Commander of the *PT-109*
   d. Dungeons and Dragons

3. When I grow up I want to be
   a. Rich
   b. Famous
   c. President of the United States
   d. A shareholder in Intel

Popular Songs
Heard Around Silicon Valley

We All Live in a Yellow Subroutine

(I Can't Get No) Staticsfaction

I Did It Pi Way

I'm in the Mode for Love

Play That Funky Music, Byte Boy

Let's Get Digital

Ain't No Modem High Enough

I Heard It through the WATS Line

Do You Know the Way to San Jose

Somewhere over the RAMbow

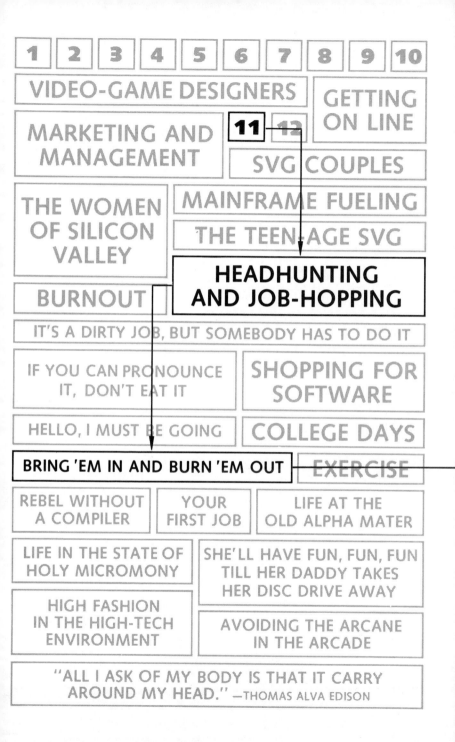

Remember when headhunters lived in darkest Africa and recruiters worked for Woody Hayes? No longer, you valuable computer commodity, you! No matter how happy you may be with your present company, the simple fact that you are a computer wiz alive in the eighties makes you fair game for roving Japanese businessmen, personnel inquiry agents, and the enlistment office of the United States Air Force. There seems to be a résumé exchange going on in the computer industry that rivals the successful chain-letter phenomenon of the 1930s. Yes, at least twice each year you'll get a call or letter or carrier pigeon from some rival company that thinks it wants your baud.

The reasons for this are many, but could include the following:

1.   The central computer for the distribution of junk mail accidentally picked up your college transcripts and sent them with the Publishers' Clearing House Sweepstakes entry forms.

2.   Someone overheard you at a party while you described your recent trip to Disneyland. You mentioned Mickey Mouse, and they thought you said you had a new design for a mini-mice plug.

3.   The companies contacting you have a use for that obscure device you developed to keep your garage door shut, which also has major applications for military aircraft.

4. While walking through the clean room on the way to the company cafeteria one day, you accidentally picked up a microchip in your trouser cuff. Later, at Happy Hour, this chip was spotted by a rival company representative and interpreted as a sign you're ready to talk turkey.

Regardless of how you're approached, there are matters of protocol that must be observed, should you be considering a transfer from your home base to another environment. To help you keep your rear out of a sling in case the new deal doesn't go through, we offer you the following handy hints:

1.   Never have lunch with more than one Japanese businessman at a time.

2.   Never totally clear off your desk.

3.   Use pay phones for personal calls.

4.   Go for interviews in the dead of night, wearing funny disguises.

5.   Do *not* activate your work terminal to print out additional copies of your résumé. Use your home computer and résumé program instead.

6.   Never mention your prospective head-hunter by name, even to your pleasure unit.

It's totally up to you, of course, if you want to leave the mother ship for an asteroid that looks like it could eventually offer you more actual board programming time and exclusive perks, not to mention a larger salary. We are merely advocating that you be cautious about any move. After all, the grass is always greener on the other side of the fetch.

POP QUIZ
Are you SVG material?

1. Nothing builds character like
   a. A Porsche in the garage
   b. A house on the beach
   c. A hot-tub attendant
   d. An office full of software

2. The man I admire most is
   a. Taller than me
   b. Richard Nixon
   c. Alex Carras
   d. Steve Wozniak

3. The woman I admire most is
   a. My mom
   b. Helen Gurley Brown
   c. Amelia Earhart
   d. The group project secretary

The company newsletter says he is taking an extended leave of absence to pursue other interests, but we all know what really happened to Ray FIFO. He went somewhere and had a meltdown, man. He burned out.

The company life expectancy of an SVG, from recruitment to retirement, averages about fifteen years in this high-tech industry. It may sound like an awfully short period of productivity, but then, how many years of late nights, vending-machine food, and exposure to low-level radiation could *you* handle? By the time the SVG hits thirty-five, the old END OF LINE is in sight. The word "terminal" takes on a whole new meaning. The ID badge is dog-eared and the beeper begins to sound more and more like the nurse buzzer in an intensive-care ward.

The first signs of burnout are subtle, but insidious. Management sends cheeky memos about the programs having so many bugs the company is thinking about merging with Black Flag. The aging SVG notices that hardly any of the younger chippies send messages to his terminal anymore, and the cute little programs down in word processing barely turn their heads when he passes by their modular office units. The dust is so thick in the bottom of the old pocket protector that it clogs up his Bic Fine Point.

And then, it happens. One morning he wakes up, looks in the mirror, and realizes he left the office the night before without turning off the high-speed printer, and his module is, by this time, loaded to the top with fifty thousand sheets of paper on which is printed ERROR X5 IOIO. That's it. The heart just isn't

in it anymore. Even the security guard knows Ray's company badge will soon be confiscated and his beeper number retired.

Retired. Not a pleasant word for someone who's main recreational activity has been working late. Somehow these wizened old souls of thirty-five learn to cope. But it isn't easy. For a retired SVG, visiting the golf course isn't a pleasant recreational activity. It's a geometric exercise in vectors and prediction of curves; it makes him immediately miss the old company 3-D graphic generator that he could use to simulate the swing of the club and the flight of the ball.

Moving to Sun City or Florida isn't an option, either. The burned-out SVG may *look* like he's as old as the other retirees, but in fact he's not (he's only thirty-six), and some instinct usually makes these mid-life codgers hang around their old haunts.

It's not unusual to see two or three of these senior chippies show up at the Burger King at about 11:30 A.M., in plenty of time to spot the younger guys from the plant coming in for lunch. After a few informal edit statements, they'll launch into a story about the good old days that bores the chippies, but is nonetheless listened to with respect and tolerance for age. Who *cares* what life was like back in 1982? The retirees do. Some of these guys remember *tubes*. The first beeper. Discs that were more faulty than floppy. Living in the past is a big part of the first few retirement years.

Slowly, though, the typical rezzed-out retiree begins to adjust. A good many eventually begin hobbies such as plastering integrated-circuit mosaics and building transistorized can openers.

For the Golden Age SVG, company retirement plans and stock buy-out packages usually provide plenty of income—enough, even, to maintain the steady supply of Baby Ruth bars and caffeinated cola drinks that Meals On Wheels ridiculously refuses to supply.

In the time warp world of Silicon Valley, these old SVGs are a little-noticed, but nonetheless valid, segment of the population. Our aging chippies are living evidence of an era of the electronics revolution gone by.

Epitaphs

We asked the question, "After the ultimate burnout, how do you want your headstone engraved?"

Some answers follow.

•

END OF
STATEMENT

•

CALL EX. 117

•

MASTERED THE
2–1 OPENING

•

HERE WAS AN
SVG
WHO BIT OFF TOO MUCH

•

HE'S DEAD, JIM

•

Key to Pop Quiz
Questions

To find out if you're SVG material, take out your pocket calculator, electronic abacus, or No. 2 pencil, and add up your points. Allot yourself 0 points for each "a" answer, one point for each "b" answer, two points for "c," and three points for "d."

0–34 points.

You belong in the pre-Columbian era. The most technological thing you probably do is rub two sticks together to start a fire.

35–60 points.

Changing the battery in your flashlight is probably a major challenge. Avoid Radio Shacks at all costs.

61–80 points.

Sure, you know what a pocket calculator is, but you probably don't use it until income-tax time. You may have potential in Management or Marketing, but you've obviously eaten too many fresh vegetables to succeed in the high-tech world.

81–102 points.

Modem to the max! You've debugged the quiz and should catch the next plane for Sunnyvale!

Glossary

Alpha flux   The number of alpha particles emitted from a surface over a period of time. In humans, a tingling, ticklish feeling causing wiggles.

Analog gate   1.   A logic gate, the output signal of which is a linear function of one or more input signals.   2.   A yard boundary, as in "a rough-hewn fence analog gate."

ANSI Abbreviation for American National Standards Institute. Also, a frustrating feeling you get when you just can't wait for something to happen.

ASCII The code used to send data by telephone, so digital messages don't get mixed up with E.T. phoning home.

Assembly program Refers to a computer program flexible enough to incorporate subroutines into the main program. What you went to in high school when the principal thought he had something to say you all had to listen to.

ATE Abbreviation for Automatic Test Equipment. Not to be confused with the past tense of "eat."

Baud A unit signaling speed equal to the number of discrete conditions or signal events per second. A euphemism for your personal mainframe.

Beeper The next best thing to being there. First used for battlefield communications during WWII, then called walkie-talkies. The ultimate SVG status symbol.

Bipolar A big white bear who swings both ways.

Bit-slice-microprocessor Just another name for Cuisinart.

Bond, Ultrasonic The star of the movie *Moonraker*.

Bubble memories   What Frank Zappa's Valley Girls have.

Calculator   What normal people use to balance their checkbooks and SVGs have built into their watches.

Charge-coupled devices   A stretched MOS with a long string of gates between the source and the drain. A sort of internal whoopee cushion.

Chip burnout   A surfer from L.A. who made B movies with Tab Hunter before abandoning the beach for college and a double-E major. And for silicon, as it were.

De-rez   Abbreviation for "deresolution," meaning to erase, zap-out, annihilate.

Edit statement   Small talk.

End sum   The love you take is equal to the love you make.

ENIAC   The first computer. Used tubes instead of chips, made up of spare parts from Frigidaires and DeSotos.

FIFO   First In, First Out memory (or action), as compared to Random Access Memory (RAM). A dude with the moves.

Fetch   1.   That portion of a computer cycle during which the location of the next instruction is determined, the instruction is taken from memory (and modified, if necessary), and then entered into the control register.   2.   What Spot does.

Floppy-disk failure   All dressed up with no place to go.

Front-end processor   Minor microprocessors that are used to interface communication termi-

nals to a host data-processing system. An object that really puts out.

Kipp relay   A cute little program's G spot.

Main program   The meat, the heart of the matter. (Your control module or mine?)

Microchip   Chip Burnout's younger brother.

M.I.T.   Massachusetts Institute of Technology. Where SVGs go to lose their virginity.

Modem   MODulation/DEModulation chip or device that enables computers and terminals to communicate. Modern–day equivalent of the dropped handkerchief.

On line   Available for access. Ready. Hot to trot.

P.G.&E.   Pacific Gas and Electric Company, without whom Silicon Valley would not exist.

Phase jitter   A type of random distortion which results in the intermittent shortening and lengthening of signals. The heebie-jeebies.

Plastic pocket protector   Status symbol for those who don't yet rate beepers.

PROM   A Programmable Read-Only Memory, as opposed to the Senior Prom.

Program   A sequence of audio signals transmitted for entertainment or information. Euphemism for girls.

Radio Shack   Convenience market for SVGs.

RAM-refresh time interval   The time between the successive refresh operations that are required to restore the charge in a dynamic memory cell. Smoking optional.

Silicon Valley   The general area below San Francisco around Sunnyvale, California, where a large concentration of semiconductor manufacturers have located their headquarters and many of their manufacturing facilities. Technology Heaven with tract housing.

Software   What Mr. Blackwell would like to see on all programs.

Spatial arena   Within body-scent range.

Subminiature DIP relays   Junior SVGs who fetch coffee and carry messages. (See *Microchip*.)

Subroutine   Necking in the car vs. getting a hotel room.

Total system dump   The electronic equivalent of the effects of Ex-Lax.

Unit   A mechanical part or module. Another euphemism for girls.

UNIVAC   ENIAC's daughter, not to be confused with carpet sweepers.

"Look out, Intel, here he comes..."

For Silicon Valley Products, write:

Bob Glazar
2102 West Earll Drive
Phoenix, Arizona 85015